Apostles, Prophets and Administrators

By Gordon Lindsay

Published By
CHRIST FOR THE NATIONS, INC.
Dallas, Texas
Revised 1994
Reprint 1994
All Rights Reserved

All Scripture NKJV unless otherwise noted.

TABLE OF CONTENTS

Introduction

Gordon Lindsay was a man of vision. He seemed to live on a higher spiritual level than many, and God prophetically revealed Himself to Gordon.

Chapter 1

The Ministry Gift of Apostle

The word *apostle* has a much wider meaning than is generally understood. The word comes from *apostolos*, which means "one sent forth, a messenger, an ambassador, a missionary." An apostle is one sent on a special mission.

Scripture shows that there are different orders of apostles. Christ Himself is spoken of as an apostle. "Therefore, holy brethren, partakers of the heavenly calling, consider the *Apostle* and High Priest of our confession, Christ Jesus" (Heb. 3:1). Christ was sent to this world by the Father on a mission of redemption. As the "Sent One," He was an Apostle.

Then came His twelve apostles. They

were given a distinct mission. The original twelve were comprised of those who were witnesses of the resurrection and ascension of the Lord (Acts 1:21,22).

The twelve apostles were given a special promise regarding their position in the kingdom at the time of the gathering of Israel. "Jesus said to them, 'Assuredly, I say to you, that in the regeneration, when the Son of Man sits on the throne of His glory, you who have followed Me will also sit on twelve thrones, judging the twelve tribes of Israel'" (Matt. 19:28).

There are those who claim that Paul was the apostle who should have taken the place of Judas. But when describing the resurrection of the Lord, Paul declared that Christ was seen "by the twelve," not by the "eleven" (I Cor. 15:5). Judas had committed suicide by that time; therefore, Matthias must have been the one indicated.

Paul does not include himself in the "twelve," for he was not yet converted.

Instead he declares of Christ in His post-resurrection manifestations: "Then *last* of all He was seen by me also, as by one born out of due time" (I Cor. 15:8).

THE THIRD GROUP OF APOSTLES

Since Paul was not a member of the original twelve, but is also called an apostle, it is evident that there is yet another group of apostles. Counting Judas, Matthias was actually the thirteenth apostle. Paul was not next in line; it was James, the Lord's brother. Paul, speaking of his visit to Jerusalem, mentions that he met James, the brother of Jesus, who was an apostle. "But I saw none of the other apostles except James, the Lord's brother" (Gal. 1:19). There were two men named James in the original twelve, but neither of them was the son of a Mary. Therefore this James was another apostle.

During Jesus' earthly ministry, James did not believe the Lord's claims. After the resurrection of Christ, he became a believer and was present at Pentecost (Acts 1:14).

Paul and Barnabus were the fifteenth and sixteenth apostles. "But when the apostles Barnabas and Paul heard this, they tore their clothes and ran in among the multitude, crying out and saying, 'Men, why are you doing these things?'" (Acts 14:14,15).

Paul calls Apollos an apostle: "Now these things, brethren, I have figuratively transferred to myself and Apollos for your sakes. ... For I think that God has displayed us, the apostles" (I Cor. 4:6,9). He was evidently linking Apollos with himself as an apostle. Therefore, Apollos is the seventeenth apostle.

In Romans 16:7 there is a remarkable declaration by Paul concerning Andronicus and Junia: "Greet Andronicus and Junia, my kinsmen and my fellow prisoners, who are of note among the apostles, who also were in Christ before me." It is clear that Andronicus and Junias were the eighteenth and nineteenth apostles.

In Philippians 2:25, the Apostle Paul speaks of Epaphroditus as his brother and companion in the Lord. He also speaks of him as "your messenger." This word "messenger" in the original Greek is "apostolos" or apostle. The Amplified Bible shows this distinction. Epaphroditus, then, is the twentieth of the apostles mentioned in the Scriptures.

FALSE APOSTLES

Since the office of an apostle is of such importance in the Church, it is not surprising that Satan, the imitator of all spiritual things, raises up false apostles. God must set apostles in the Church. Man cannot do it. He who usurps the position of an apostle is a false apostle. Some attempted to do this in the Early Church and were denounced as false apostles. Speaking of these Paul said, "For such are false apostles, deceitful workers, transforming themselves into apostles of Christ. And no wonder! For Satan himself transforms himself into an angel of light. Therefore it is no great thing if his ministers also transform themselves into ministers of righteousness, whose end will be according to their works" (II Cor. 11:13-15).

A false apostle is identified first by the fact that the person appoints himself to the office of an apostle. The second sign is that he fails to produce the works of an apostle. The Early Church took note of those who claimed apostleship, but who in fact were false apostles. They were tried and exposed as liars so that they would not be able to lead astray the sheep of the Church of Christ.

It is evident that the office of an apostle is needed in the Church today. But history shows the danger of any man calling himself an apostle. Groups attempting to restore apostolic functions by electing apostles have merely exposed their own folly. Sometimes those claiming to be apostles sometimes have, at the beginning, manifested a generous spirit. But they soon became arbitrary and sectarian and usually bring people under bondage. When James and John sought to get a preferred position among the apostles with the help of their mother, Jesus reproved them. "You know that the rulers of the Gentiles lord it over them, and those who are great exercise authority over them. Yet it shall not be so among you; but whoever desires to become great among you, let him be your servant. And whoever desires to be first among you, let him be your slave — just as the Son of Man did not come to be served, but to serve, and to give His life a ransom for many" (Matt. 20:25-28).

TRUE APOSTLES

True apostles first manifest their apostolic ministry by humility. The ministry that God has given them is revealed by their works rather than by a public proclamation of the office. One can do the work of an apostle without calling himself one. The office of an apostle is to a great extent misunderstood. Many think it is an elevation to a position of authority whereby one may rule over God's people. The words of Jesus just quoted show the error in such a concept. When a person does the work of an apostle, then his ministry will become recognized.

The humility of John the Baptist is an example for God's ministers today. John said, "He must increase, but I must decrease" (Jn. 3:30). God sent this messenger forth "in the spirit and power of Elijah, 'to turn the hearts of the fathers to the children,' and the disobedient to the wisdom of the just, to make ready a people prepared for the LORD" (Lk. 1:17).

"Among those born of women there has not risen one greater than John the Baptist" (Matt. 11:11). These words came from Jesus. But when they asked John if he was Elijah, he answered that he was not

(Jn. 1:21). Yet Jesus said concerning his ministry, "If you are willing to receive it, he is Elijah who is to come" (Matt. 11:14). It is evident that one does not have to assume a title in order to fulfill a Scriptural ministry. In fact, assuming such a title might do more harm than good. Even Jesus very cautiously revealed His Messiahship. Public proclamation of it could have rallied the people to Him in a manner that would hinder His mission.

Another distinguishing feature of an apostle is that he is a "sent one" and a "missionary." Anyone who claims to have the office of an apostle and has no burden for the lost is not a true apostle.

THE MARKS OF AN APOSTLE'S MINISTRY

1. **An apostle will have a burden for the welfare of the whole Church.** Of course, he cannot actually minister to all members of the body. But his burden will be for the Church of Christ as

a whole. This is seen in Ephesians 4:11-16:

And He Himself gave some to be apostles, some prophets, some evangelists, and some pastors and teachers, for the equipping of the saints for the work of ministry, for *the edifying of the body of Christ,* till we all come to the unity of the faith and the knowledge of the Son of God, to a perfect man, to the measure of the stature of the fullness of Christ; that we should no longer be children, tossed to and fro and carried about with every wind of doctrine, by the trickery of men, in the cunning craftiness by which they lie in wait to deceive, but, speaking the truth in love, may grow up in all things into Him who is the head — Christ — from whom the whole body, joined and knit together by what every joint supplies, according to the effective working by which every part does its share, causes growth of the body for the edifying of itself in love.

A study of the above passage reveals that the responsibility of an apostle — as well as that of a prophet, evangelist, teacher or pastor — is for the whole body of Christ. A true apostle will intuitively manifest an interest and will labor for the edifying of the whole body until all members "come to the unity of the faith."

2. **He will not have a covetous spirit or be a seeker after financial gain.** Judas, one of the original twelve, not only disqualified himself, but destroyed his own soul by using his position for personal gain. He was treasurer of the apostolate, and carried the money bag. Before he committed the climactic act of treachery by betraying Christ for 30 pieces of silver,

he had become an habitual thief. When Mary poured the ointment on Jesus, Judas was indignant and demanded to know why the ointment was not sold and the money given to the poor. The Scriptures reveal that Judas said this, "not that he cared for the poor, but because he was a thief, and had the money box; and he used to take what was put in it" (Jn. 12:6).

A true apostle will not have a covetous spirit. He may, in the interest of the kingdom, become responsible for handling large sums of money, as the apostles were when the multitude sold their possessions and laid them at the apostles' feet (Acts 4:34,35). But he will be a faithful steward, and never take money that was given for the work of the kingdom. The story of Judas, given such prominence in the Scriptures, is of deep significance.

3. **True apostles do not seek the glory of men.** Jesus said, "How can you

believe, who receive honor from one another, and do not seek the honor that comes from the only God?" (Jn. 5:44). The mark of a false apostle is coveting human adulation rather than honor from God. Diotrephes is an example of one who desired preeminence. He refused to recognize the true apostles, "prating against us with malicious words. ... Putting them out of the church" (III Jn. 10,11). Diotrephes, who sought to divide the body of Christ because of personal ambition, revealed himself as a false leader.

Paul said of his own conduct, "Nor did we seek glory from men, either from you or from others, when we might have made demands as apostles of Christ" (I Thes. 2:6).

An apostle, far from finding his ministry a popular one, may on occasion be faced with severe persecution. Consequently, he must possess unusual grace and humility if he is to be successful in fulfilling his mission. Paul declared, "For I think that God has displayed us, the apostles, last, as men condemned to death; for we have been made a spectacle to the world, both to angels and to men" (I Cor. 4:9).

It is apparent that only those who can die to personal ambition will be successful in such an office. Those who seek after such an office for the prominence and honor that it might give are revealing they are unqualified for the office, regardless of what other talents they possess.

4. **An apostle possesses a supernatural ministry.** An apostle's work is a supernatural one and he must be fully armed with the power and gifts of the Spirit. He can accomplish his work in no other way. To profess to be an apostle without signs following would be to mark one's self as a false apostle.

In the Early Church, the apostles preached the Gospel of Christ with great signs and wonders. "And with great power the apostles gave witness to the resurrection of the Lord Jesus. And great grace was upon them all" (Acts 4:33). In the next chapter, a similar statement is made. "And through the hands of the apostles many signs and wonders were done among the people" (Acts 5:12).

Paul associated the ministry of the supernatural with the ministry of a true apostle. In writing to the Corinthians he says: "Truly the signs of an apostle were accomplished among you with all perseverance, in signs and wonders and mighty deeds" (II Cor. 12:12). But even a supernatural ministry in itself is not enough to qualify one as an apostle. Evangelists, prophets and even deacons possessed such a ministry in the Early Church. Notice in the above Scripture that an apostle should minister among the people "with all perseverance." That means he must patiently minister to God's people, not seeking to vindicate his own honor, but laboring for the good of the body of Christ.

5. **Apostles minister discipline supernaturally.** Another mark of an apostle is that when severe discipline is necessary in the Church, he will minister it supernaturally. When discipline is given out in the usual manner, it leaves the individual free to incite opposition against the Church. The methods used by the apostles in the Early Church kept it pure and free of evil elements.

The immoral man in the Corinthian Church is an example of necessary discipline. Paul told the believers in Corinth that there was sin in their midst, and they needed to deal with it accordingly. A man was living in sexual immorality with his father's wife. Although Paul was not present in body, he was present in spirit and in the name of the Lord Jesus Christ, along with Paul's spirit, they were to "deliver such a one to Satan for the destruction of the flesh, that his spirit may be saved in the day of the Lord Jesus" (I Cor. 5:5). They were to purge this man from their midst in order to prevent the leaven of sin spreading throughout the entire body. "A little leaven leavens the whole lump" (I Cor. 5:6).

6. **An apostle is "a messenger;" he is one "sent" on a mission.** His vision is to evangelize for Christ. He has been sent of God to help turn the nations to God.

Christ in His Great Commission said, "Preach the gospel to every creature." He also said, "And this gospel of the kingdom will be preached in all the world as a witness to all the nations, and then the end will come" (Matt. 24:14). It is unthinkable that an apostle or any other ministry set in the body of Christ should have any vision other than this.

7. **The apostle will teach sound doctrine.** Since the work of an apostle is to bring people into a knowledge of the Son of God so that they will "no longer be children, tossed to and fro and carried about with every wind of doctrine" (Eph. 4:14), he will be sound in the faith and in purity of doctrine. The great Apostle Paul repeatedly urged Timothy and Titus to hold to sound doctrine, and to avoid those things that excite curiosity and vain wrangling and do not edify the Church.

Chapter 2

The Ministry Gift of Prophet

The ministry of prophecy is an integral part of the New Testament Church. There were at least three prophets in the Corinthian Church (I Cor. 14:29). This ministry is second in importance and order in the body of Christ. The purposes and characteristics of this ministry are declared in the Scriptures:

1. **A prophet possesses a definite gift of prophecy.** There are certain other qualifications. Jesus had a ministry of prophecy and therefore referred to Himself as a prophet (Lk. 4:24; 13:33). Jesus of course was far more than a prophet.

2. **A true prophet will show proper**

humility and will be amenable to advice from other ministry gifts set in the Church.

If anyone thinks himself to be a prophet or spiritual, let him acknowledge that the things which I write to you are the commandments of the Lord (I Cor. 14:37).

3. **While the gift of prophecy is infallible when the prophet is perfectly yielded to the Spirit, New Testament prophets are not to be considered infallible.** "Let two or three prophets speak, and let the others *judge*" (I Cor. 14:29). It is quite proper to judge all prophecy in the light of the Scriptures.

4. **One of the ministries of a prophet is to exhort and strengthen (Acts 15:32).**

But he who prophesies speaks edification and exhortation and comfort to men (I Cor. 14:3).

5. **Another ministry of the prophet in the Church is the foreseeing of events of the future.** Agabus forewarned the church at Antioch that a great famine was coming upon the world. The Church at Antioch was then able to quickly send relief to their brothers and sisters in Judea. In the days of Claudius Caesar the famine actually came to pass as was prophesied (Acts 11:27-30).

6. **The prophet, along with others with ministry gifts, is to pray over and lay hands on those being separated for a special ministry (Acts 13:3).**

7. **Prophets, together with the apostles, are a part of the foundation of the New Testament Church.**

   The Apostle John gives a warning concerning false prophets:

   > Beloved, do not believe every spirit, but test the spirits, whether they are of God; because many

false prophets have gone out into
the world (I Jn. 4:1).

Prophets will be recogized by their
fruit. A true prophet has the Spirit of
Christ. Their works will be of the
Spirit of Christ. False prophets are revealed at some point by their nature;
though clothed in sheep's clothing,
they are self-promoting and may even
be cruel and relentless.

THE NATURE OF PROPHETIC MINISTRY

In the Old Testament, the prophetic
ministry was essentially *foretelling*. In the
New Testament, the emphasis is on
forthtelling. When Adam and Eve were
placed in the Garden of Eden, God con-
versed with them directly. That communion was broken by their disobedience. In
a certain sense, the gift of prophecy re-
stores that direct communion.

The prophetic gift has many vari-
ations. It may be exhortational; it may

take the form of song or poetry as in the Psalms; or it may on occasion reveal future events. The gift has varied operations, and in some instances may be a vehicle for other gifts such as the word of wisdom, the word of knowledge or the discerning of spirits.

Prophecy relating to the future is of two distinct kinds. Some prophecies are unconditional; for example, the Abrahamic covenant or the Messianic prophecies. Others are conditional, such as Isaiah's warning of Hezekiah's impending death (II Ki. 20:1-6) or Jonah's pronouncement of judgment on Nineveh (Jon. 3:3-10). Fulfillment of unconditional prophecies are not dependent upon man or his responses. *Fulfillment of conditional prophecies, however, does depend on the response — the obedience or disobedience — of the persons to whom they are addressed.*

There is a difference between revelation prophecy and exhortational prophecy. In exhortational prophecy, the Spirit of God takes over the person's subconscious mind and from his storehouse selects, rearranges and anoints certain truths for the edification of the hearers. Revelation prophecy involves a greater yielding to the Spirit. Exhortational prophecy is more prevalent and usually is the kind manifested in public services (I Cor. 14:26).

There is a hunger in the hearts of people for revelation prophecy. Nevertheless, because of the complexity of the gift, certain safeguards are important in its operation. The gift of prophecy involves the merging of the human and the divine, the finite with the infinite, the imperfect with the perfect.

TRUE PROPHECY

"For the testimony of Jesus is the spirit of prophecy" (Rev. 19:10). True prophecy always points to Christ, His deity, His ministry, His purpose in coming into the world and His return to earth. Alleged prophetic gifts that engage in telling fortunes, divining mysteries, predicting the outcome of political events, locating lost articles, etc., betray the fact that they are something other than the biblical gift. The true gift of prophecy is not to be confused with fortune-telling, extrasensory perception, clairvoyance and other psychic manifestations. It may, however, give guidance and counsel at times. People should first search the Scriptures before looking for further guidance. Moreover, just as some people misinterpret Scripture, some misinterpret prophecy. Spiritual discernment is needed to understand either.

Old Testament prophets on occasion assumed the time of fulfillment of their prophecies would be sooner than they were in actuality. Some make that mistake today. The Bible speaks of apocalyptic judgments taking place during "the day of the LORD" that "is great and very terrible" (Joel 2:11). That time is not far off, but it has not yet come. When people are given the impression that some catastrophic event is to happen immediately and it fails to take place, they are prone to lose confidence in the gift altogether.

God gives certain kinds of guidance by means of the revelation gifts. The warning received by Paul when he was on his way to Jerusalem (Acts 20:22,23) came thusly. Even so, the prophecy had to be correctly interpreted. Paul interpreted the prophecy as a warning of what would happen to him if he went to Jerusalem; he did not see it as a prohibition. The Apostle went on to his destination, apparently in the will of God, although events transpired just as they had been prophesied.

The gift is not intended as a vehicle to establish new doctrine. Peter warned of those who will come into the Church with "destructive heresies" (II Pet. 2:1) which can lead to great confusion. Some of the most serious heresies owe their origin to the "private interpretation" of some self-styled prophet.

Despite these problems, we sorely need the inspiration and revelation gifts in operation in the Church. May God give us discernment to distinguish between the true and the false. Paul commands, "Do not despise prophecies. Test all things; hold fast what is good" (I Thes. 5:20,21).

Chapter 3

The Ministry Gift of Administrator

Besides apostles and prophets, there are many other ministries which the Holy Spirit has set within the body of Christ. Included are: "Teachers, after that miracles, then gifts of healings, helps, administrations, varieties of tongues" (I Cor. 12:28). Helps, for example may include a great variety of less spectacular, but nonetheless important ministries. All of these ministries must function freely within the body. Does the office of an administrator have the element of the supernatural in it? Or is it a ministry that functions entirely through the use of natural methods, like those used in the governing of human organizations or institutions? Scripture is clear as to the purpose of this ministry.

A fundamental truth of the New Testament is that every believer is a priest. In Old Testament days, believers had access to God chiefly through someone else. All members of the body of Christ should commune personally with God and not be dependent on someone else. Peter declares:

> But you are a chosen generation,
> a royal priesthood, a holy nation,
> His own special people, that you
> may proclaim the praises of Him
> who called you out of darkness
> into His marvelous light (I Pet.
> 2:9).

Nevertheless, the New Testament believer is not to be an "individualist," but interdependent with other members of the body of Christ.

We are under obligation to cooperate with other members of the body as well as to be subject to the Head, Who is Christ. God has placed administration in the Church, for He is a God of order and not of confusion. This ministry of administration has a supernatural element, just like other ministries of the body of Christ.

The New Testament speaks with some detail of administration in the local church, but little of what goes beyond the local church. It is evident that the New Testament purposely omits giving detailed instructions concerning any universal church government. The Church would extend through many centuries. During this long period, circumstances and conditions would go through many changes. The Word gives us a full revelation as far as principles are concerned, but definite methods of organization are not specified. What might work best at one time might not at another. What might be best for one group might not be for another. This is clearly seen in the order set up in the first Church at Jerusalem.

THE EARLY COMMUNAL CHURCH

The first Church was a communal church. The people sold their possessions and had all things in common. Few today advocate that we should return to that form of organization. Attempts to revive a communal church have had varying degrees of success. Many attempts were not very successful, but in the Early Church it worked well for a time and apparently it carried the blessing of God. We have no information that implies it was specifically authorized by God, however. There are reasons why a communal church was successful at that time:

1. It was a voluntary arrangement. No one was forced to sell his property and give it to the apostles (Acts 5:4).
2. All the people were filled with the Holy Spirit and their hearts were filled with great love.

3. The Church was under severe persecution. Some believers were martyred, others thrown into prison. Such persecution drives people together. The multitude living together experienced a sense of security they would not have felt if they had been isolated from one another at that critical time. Today many Jews in Israel live in communal settlements, especially in areas where they are subject to Arab raids.

4. The apostles exercised divine discipline, removing wicked persons from their midst that might have destroyed the purity and unity of the Church. This brought great fear on the Church and prevented the infiltration of evil (Acts 5:11-13).

5. Christians had been warned about what was ahead. Jesus had told them that judgment was coming on Jerusalem; the city was to be destroyed (Lk. 13:35; 19:43,44; 21:20-24). And this was to come to pass in their generation

(Matt. 23:36). Knowing these things, it is not surprising that they felt a strong urge to dispose of their property and invest it in the kingdom of God. Judgment came in the years A.D. 66-70 about the time of Paul's martyrdom. But the Christians, having been warned beforehand, escaped to Pella.

BIBLICAL PRINCIPLES

While it is true that God did not lay down an absolute form of organization in either a local church or interchurch system (else we would have to follow that of the communal church at Jerusalem), some administration is necessary. But whatever the method chosen, it must not violate any of the principles of the body of Christ. These divine principles must always supersede any human arrangements that might compromise these principles. In other words, any ecclesiastical laws that compromise the headship of Christ are unconstitutional.

1. The Church must acknowledge the principle of the supreme headship of Christ. There is no place for a vicar of Christ.

2. It must acknowledge the fellowship of the whole body of Christ. That is, no group may restrict fellowship on the lines of its own organization. That would be dividing the body of Christ.

3. It must acknowledge all the ministries which God sets in the Church. It should not deny initiative to those whom God has called to special ministries in the body (I Cor. 12:28).

4. Doctrinally, it should stand for the principles of the doctrine of Christ (Heb. 6:1,2).

5. It should be flexible and responsive to revival when, where and how God should send it. Historically, revivals have come through individuals. Churches may greatly benefit from such visitations if they are sensitive to the moving of the Spirit of God.

Paul declares that there are "diversities of operations." Therefore, it is evident that every person's ministry will in some degree differ from another's. All ministries are needed in order to edify the Church and to bring it into holy unity and fellowship. Certain ministers, because of the ministries they possess and their burden for the whole body of Christ, will be recognized as pillars in the Church (Gal. 2:9).

But even these men, Paul hastens to show, are not infallible; they are subject to making mistakes (Gal. 2:11-14). Peter on one occasion was about to give way to Jewish pressure for a separation of fellowship between the Jewish Church and the gentile Church. Paul insisted that this fellowship not be broken.

DISCIPLINE IN THE EARLY CHURCH

Ordinary methods of discipline were

exercised in the Early Church. But when ordinary methods failed to preserve the unity of the body of Christ, then discipline was exercised supernaturally. This was true in the punishment of Ananias and Sapphira (Acts 5: 1-11). Another example is the case of Hymenaeus and Alexander (I Tim. 1:20). They denied one of the principles of the doctrine of Christ — the doctrine of resurrection (II Tim. 2:18). The unity of the Early Church was preserved.

As we have seen, God set helps and administrations in the Church. Specific methods of their ministrations are not given in detail in the New Testament. But however they functioned, they were to work in harmony and accord with the other ministry gifts.

CHURCH ORGANIZATION IN THE WILDERNESS

Moses, under the heavy responsibility of leadership of the people of the Church in the wilderness, was advised by his father-in-law to appoint others to work under him. Moses followed the advice of his father-in-law (Ex. 18). This form of government that was set up completely failed. In the course of time we find Moses confessing that he was about to break under the burden (Num. 11:14,15).

It is commonly thought that Jethro's advice was wrong. But is that altogether true? The principle of deputation of work is sound. What was wrong was that the men who had first been appointed as elders were not anointed of the Spirit. Consequently, they could only fail in their task, just as those of any church organization today who are without the anointing of God upon their lives will fail. God took some of the Spirit that was upon Moses and put it upon 70 elders (Num. 11:16-29), making them qualified for their task. These may well have been the same elders.

A certain amount of organization is

necessary where men labor together for a common purpose. Organization is a working agreement between brethren. But spiritual tasks require men anointed by the Holy Spirit. Without this they are sure to fail. The ministry of administration is a supernatural ministry, just as are gifts of healings. This office must have the anointing of God upon it, just as other supernatural gifts, such as the word of wisdom and the word of knowledge must have, if they are to be successful in their operation. Above all, those with the gift of administration must truly recognize the headship of Christ over the body.

THE LOCAL CHURCHES

When Christ sent His messages by John to the local churches in Asia Minor (Rev. 2,3), He called them to an accounting. Each church was responsible directly to the Lord for its conduct. Thus the headship of Christ was maintained in the body.

In the Early Church, elders were

appointed as overseers of the Church (Acts 20:28; I Tim. 5:17). They were also called bishops (I Tim. 3:1), and were subject to certain qualifications. Under them were deacons, whose duties were more in the temporal sphere (Acts 6:1-7). These were appointed by the elders after they had been nominated by the church.

FELLOWSHIP EXTENDED BEYOND THE LOCAL CHURCH

Lack of transportation in the days of the Early Church limited fellowship between the various churches. Yet fellowship was maintained as much as possible under the circumstances. When an important question came up in the church at Antioch, the leaders went to Jerusalem, where the elders and apostles came together to consider the matter and to make a decision (Acts 15). When Peter and Barnabas thought to withdraw fellowship from the gentile Church, Paul sharply rebuked them.

There was no elaborate organization in the churches in the days of the apostles. The elders, however, came together on occasion for mutual counsel. Paul commissioned Timothy to travel and ordain elders in certain churches. The Early Church was organized to care for the poor, the widows and to do missionary work. The autonomy of the local church in apostolic days is strongly evident.

THERE WAS A STANDARD OF FELLOWSHIP

The fellowship was not all inclusive. People had to meet a certain standard to be accepted in the fellowship. Immoral persons were not permitted in that fellowship; neither were those who were unruly or did not walk according to the traditions set forth by the apostles (II Thes. 3:6). Domineering and sectarian leaders were excluded (III Jn. 9-11). Fellowship was also based on acceptance of the doctrine of Christ (II Jn. 9-11).

In the Early Church it was common for an evangelist or minister to carry letters of recommendation when going into an area where his ministry was not known or there was a possibility that it would be in question (Acts 15:22-31). The principle was that a person should carry a letter of recommendation from a previous field of labor when going into another. Throughout the letters of Paul, we find statements in which he recommended the ministry of some and warned the churches against others.

CERTAIN MINISTRIES SET IN THE CHURCH

We are told specifically that God set certain ministries or ministry-gifts in the Church:

> And He Himself gave some to be apostles, some prophets, some evangelists, and some pastors

and teachers, for the equipping of the saints for the work of ministry, for the edifying of the body of Christ, till we all come to the unity of the faith and the knowledge of the Son of God, to a perfect man, to the measure of the stature of the fullness of Christ; that we should no longer be children, tossed to and fro and carried about with every wind of doctrine (Eph. 4:11-14).

These are the ministry gifts that Christ has given to the Church as a whole. These gifts are also listed in I Corinthians 12, along with ministries that include persons in the Church who are not actual elders:

Now you are the body of Christ, and members individually. And God has appointed these in the church: first apostles, second prophets, third teachers, after that miracles, then gifts of healings, helps, administrations, varieties of tongues (I Cor. 12:27,28).

THE PLACE OF DENOMINATIONS

What place does a denomination hold in the New Testament Church? Are denominations Scriptural or unscriptural? We should ask what a denomination is. A denomination is something that has been "denominated," or in other words, given a name. R.E. McAlister sums up the matter when he says:

> Any group of Christians whether large or small, whether local, national or international, who are designated by a name, a doctrine, a form of worship, a policy of church government or united in any common cause such as evangelism or missionary work is a denomination. To be associated with a group of God's children who stand for the full Gospel,

whether in a local assembly or in a larger fellowship which takes on national or international proportions, is commendable.

The first denomination of the Christian dispensation was called Disciples of Christ. In the four Gospels and the book of Acts, this group is referred to by name about two hundred and fifty times. ... The second designation of God's people in this dispensation was Christian. The disciples were first called Christians at Antioch (Acts 11:26). Since that time, several hundred denominations have taken the name and called themselves Christians. The Christian Church, Christian Missionary Alliance, Evangelical Christian and many others are still familiar names, which designate groups of God's children as denominations. It remained for the Apostle Paul, by divine revelation, to bring to the world the truth of the body of Christ which is the Church. From then on the name "Church" came into prominence and that name is used over one hundred times in the New Testament. These local churches were associated together and took on national, international and universal proportions. In this affiliation or association they were designated as "the general assembly and church of the firstborn" (Heb. 12:23).

As time went on, the Church took on national and international proportions. In keeping with this expansion and extension, the recognition of one universal Church as members of the body of Christ was retained. At the same time there was a local,

national and international recognized affiliation and organization to the point of efficiency and
economy. Each assembly was a
self-governing unit, in a great
universal brotherhood of united
churches in Christ.

Rev. McAlister's statement is a fair
one. A church may function as a church
independent of all other churches. But for
many reasons, it is advisable that
churches find a basis for cooperative fellowship. In these days when swift transportation allows for the intermingling of
people from various churches in a measure greater than any other time in history,
it is urgently necessary that some basis of
fellowship between all true believers be
found. As Christ showed in John 17:21,
the unity of the Church is necessary if the
world is to believe that Jesus is the Christ.

Rev. McAlister adds this in his statement concerning religious organizations:
"Some denominations and sects are

decidedly unscriptural and modern." One can scarcely deny this. A falling away from spiritual power in a religious organization usually results in the usurpation of the headship of Christ. Therefore, it is absolutely essential that this headship be kept inviolate. A religious organization can by a simple test ascertain if it is in harmony with the will of God: Does it recognize the whole body of Christ by lip service or in reality? Is it a fellowship that encourages the unity and harmony of all members of the body of Christ, or does the denomination regard its organization mainly as a defense against competition?

Recognition of the supremacy of the headship of Christ is necessary for the attainment of a universal fellowship of God's people. Only when a universal fellowship is attained can we say that we have given Christ pre-eminence. For only when the members of the body are working in complete harmony and unity can it be said that the head has full control over the body.

BIBLE SCHOOLS AROUND THE WORLD
Dallas • Jamaica • Germany
Canada • Hawaii • Argentina

CFNI is more than just a Bible school; it's a spiritual experience! Since the school's founding in 1970, over 23,000 students of all ages and backgrounds from every state and 45 nations have been prepared to minister the Gospel.

CHRIST FOR THE NATIONS MAGAZINE

In continual publication for over 46 years, *Christ For The Nations* magazine is one of the most enduring Spirit-filled publications in the world. Dynamic articles and prophetic reports are featured in each issue. The magazine also reports on CFN's upcoming seminars, retreats and tours.

A free subscription is available upon request in the U.S. and Canada. (Due to high mailing costs, foreign subscriptions require $10.00 per year.)

CHRIST FOR THE NATIONS
– TOUCHING LIVES AROUND THE WORLD –

CHRIST FOR THE NATIONS, INC.–
A 46-YEAR HISTORY IN WORLD MISSIONS

In 1948 Gordon and Freda Lindsay founded Christ For The Nations, a multidenominational missionary organization. Since its inception, this ministry has continually grown and today works in 120 nations, publishes books in 75 languages, aids in worldwide relief projects and assists native congregations with their church buildings. The emphasis of the organization is to obey Christ's Great Commission.

NATIVE CHURCH PROGRAM

Since 1962, CFN's Native Church Program has helped finance the building of nearly 10,000 foreign churches for needy congregations in developing nations, establishing indigenous lighthouses of the Gospel throughout the world.

LITERATURE CRUSADE

Gordon Lindsay authored over 250 books; some 45 million copies are in print. The CFN Literature Crusade books consist of 13 books dealing with the topics of salvation, prayer, the Holy Spirit, healing and other important aspects of being a Christian. They are distributed in Third–World countries.

CFN RELIEF PROJECTS

Famine, drought, earthquake, fire, war. Every year, CFN responds to the cry of the needy, providing food, blankets, clothing, medical supplies and Gospel literature to Third-World nations.

WHY CHOOSE CHRIST FOR THE NATIONS INSTITUTE?

> A balanced curriculum for dynamic living plus prayerfully selected, anointed, charismatic teachers.

> Low tuition (comparable schools charge much more than CFNI).

> Classes for all ages — (⅓ of the student body are single men, ⅓ single women, ⅓ married) offering a 2-year program (3rd year option). Classes: 8:00 a.m.–12 noon. (85% of students work off campus.)

> Variety of elective classes early in the mornings, afternoon and evenings, including computer courses.

> A Jewish Studies Department.

> Splendid music program includes an orchestra and two choirs. it also offers instruction in voice, piano, organ, drums, wind instruments, tambourine and guitar.

> Overseas summer outreaches for students, plus 22 local student ministries.

> On-campus ACE academy (K5 thru Grade 12) for children of students. Free nursery.

> 76-acre campus with inexpensive housing for all. Tennis court, gym, track and swimming pools.

> CFNI credits are accepted by an ever-increasing number of colleges for those wanting to continue on for a degree.

Some features apply only to CFNI — Dallas.